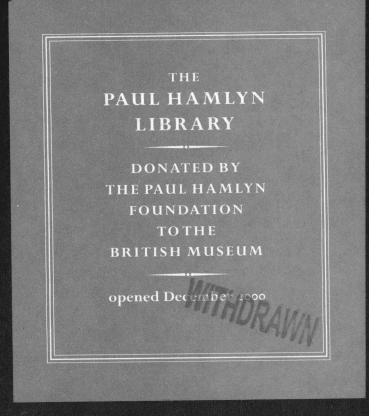

Books in the Linkers series

Homes discovered through Art & Technology
Homes discovered through Geography
Homes discovered through History
Homes discovered through Science

Myself discovered through Art & Technology
Myself discovered through Geography
Myself discovered through History
Myself discovered through Science

Toys discovered through Art & Technology
Toys discovered through Geography
Toys discovered through History
Toys discovered through Science

Water discovered through Art & Technology
Water discovered through Geography
Water discovered through History
Water discovered through Science

Food discovered through Art & Technology
Food discovered through Geography
Food discovered through History
Food discovered through Science

Journeys discovered through Art & Technology
Journeys discovered through Geography
Journeys discovered through History
Journeys discovered through Science

First published 1997 A&C Black (Publishers) Limited
35 Bedford Row, London WC1R 4JH

ISBN 0-7136-4764-7
A CIP catalogue record for this book is available from the British Library.

Commissioned photographs by Zul Mukhida
Design by Jean Wheeler

Acknowledgements

Advertising Archives; 13 (right), 15 (right), 18 (left), 19, Beamish; 4 (both), 5, 6, 7 (both), 9 (right), 10, 14, 20, 21 (both), 22 (both), 23, National Trust for Scotland; cover, Odhams Press Ltd.; 15 (left), Robert Opie; 11 (left), 18 (left), Sainsbury's Archives; 8, 9 (left).

Every effort has been made to contact copyright holders of any material reproduced in this book.
Any omissions will be rectified in future printings if notice is given to the Publisher.

Printed and bound in Italy by L.E.G.O.

641.3009BRY.

Food

discovered through
History

Karen Bryant-Mole

<u>Contents</u>

A & C Black • London

Food

This is a meal that you might eat today.
For the main course, there is a slice of pizza and some peas.
For dessert, there is a creamy, fruit yoghurt.

The pizza was bought, ready-made, in a supermarket.
The peas were frozen.
The yoghurt came in a sealed pot.

This is a meal that your grandparents, or even your great-grandparents, might have eaten.
There is a meat pudding with boiled potatoes, carrots and parsnips for the main course and rice pudding for dessert.

The meat pudding would have been made at home.
The vegetables might have been grown in the garden.
The rice pudding would have been baked in the oven.

Over time, the ways in which food is grown, sold and cooked have changed.
This book will show you some of the changes that have happened during the past one hundred years.

Farms

People

One hundred years ago, producing food on a farm was hard, slow work.
The farm workers on the right are planting seeds in a field.
The horses are pulling harrows, which rake the earth.
A man is scattering seeds by hand.

Improvements

This picture was taken in the 1910s.
The farmer is about to spread a special product called artificial fertiliser on his field.
Artificial fertilisers and chemicals called pesticides helped farmers to get more crops from the same amount of land.

Machines

Machines, like this 1920s tractor, made a big difference to farmwork.

Tractors helped people to do the work more quickly. This tractor is pulling a reaper-binder, which cuts and bundles up corn.

Transporting food

From the farm

A hundred years ago, some foods were delivered straight from the farm to people's homes.

The milk that was produced on this farm was put into large milk churns. Then it was taken to people's homes by horse and cart.

Canals

Food and other goods were often transported around the country in horse-drawn barges, along canals.

The canals passed through towns and connected up with rivers.

Many barges, like the one in the 1900s photograph on the right, also had a sail to help them along.

Trains

The picture on the left was taken in the 1920s.

The workers are unloading bananas from a goods wagon on a train. The bananas would have been brought to Britain by boat. They will make the next part of their journey by horse and cart. Today, food is usually carried around the country by lorry.

Shopping

We buy most of our food from shops.

Assistants

A hundred years ago, people didn't have freezers or fridges, so they usually went shopping every day. Many shops, like the one below, displayed the food, unwrapped, on long counters.
An assistant would weigh out the amount the customer wanted and then wrap it up in paper.

Delivering food

Lots of shops offered to deliver food to people's homes. This 1920s picture shows a delivery boy with his bike.

Food was also delivered by horse-drawn carts and, later, by vans.

Self-service shops

By the 1950s, many foods were sold in packets, boxes, bottles or tins.

In the shop on the left, people picked the food they wanted from the shelves. This was called 'self-service'.

Today, a lot of people shop in supermarkets.

Most of the food is ready-packaged but you can still have some foods weighed out for you.

9

Choice

Today, we can choose from a wider range of foods than in the past.

Seasons

Some foods, such as raspberries, are only produced in certain seasons.
In the past, food was only available at the time it was produced.
The signs in this shop window tell customers that lamb is now available.
With today's freezers, we can have almost any food at any time of year.

Rationing

During the Second World War, some types of food were in very short supply and so rationing was introduced.

Rationed foods included milk, meat, sugar, bacon, sweets, cheese, jam, eggs, tea, butter, margarine and lard.

This picture shows you how much of each food one person could buy each week.

Varieties

As time goes on, more and more varieties of food can be bought.

A hundred years ago, porridge was one of the few breakfast cereals available.

Today, there are over a hundred different types and makes of cereal to choose from.

Storing food

Once food has been bought, it has to be stored.

Larder
A hundred years ago, people would have stored their food in an airy, cool cupboard, called a larder.
Bread, flour and other dry foods were often kept in storage tins like these.
They stopped mice or insects getting at the food.

Fridges

The 1950s advert on the right shows a man surprising his wife with her first fridge.

Earlier fridges were very expensive but by the fifties they had become more affordable.

Foods like milk, butter and meat stayed fresh for much longer in a fridge than they did in a larder.

Fitted kitchens

By the 1960s, fitted kitchens were very popular.

The matching cupboards were used to store tins and dry food, such as cereals, flour and sugar.

The stainless steel sink and Formica worktop were easy to wipe clean with a cloth.

Keeping food

There are many ways of keeping food for longer and which stop it from going bad. This is called preserving food.

Canning

This 1920s advert shows some canned food.
Meat, fruit and vegetables were all available in cans but they were much more expensive than fresh food.

Freezing

The woman in the 1950s picture on the right is shopping for frozen food.

Instead of having large freezers, as we have today, most people only had a freezer compartment at the top of their fridge.

1. For oven bottling pick fruit and put into the jars. Pack as evenly as possible.

3 lb. pl
Cut the fru
Crack the s
Simmer the
the fruit is t
to the boil.
 Boil rapid
tested on a
and tie dow

Tinned frui
jars are exp
doing a litt
Ordinary ja
of special to
them.
 Vegetable
this can be d
market.
 Bottling f
in a sugar sy
can be use
quality ingr

Pickling and bottling

Pickling and bottling were popular ways of preserving food at home.

This 1950s cookery book showed people how to bottle fruit. Bottled foods were preserved in water or a sugary syrup. Pickled foods were preserved in vinegar. Both were kept in tightly-sealed jars.

Utensils

The tools we use in the kitchen to prepare food are called kitchen utensils.

Mincers
Today we buy meat ready-minced from supermarkets and butchers' shops. A hundred years ago, most households had a mincer, like the one in the picture above.

Can openers
The old-fashioned can opener below was harder to use than our modern can openers. First, the sharp point was stabbed into the lid. Then the blade had to be worked all the way around.

Lemon juicers

The wooden tool above is
a lemon juicer. It was pushed into
half a lemon and then twisted.
Today's juicers are often made
from plastic.

Tea

In the past, tea was always made with
loose tea leaves.
It had to be poured through a strainer.
Today, most people use tea bags, which
let the flavour out but keep
the tea leaves in.

Vegetable mashers

These are both vegetable mashers.
One is made from wood. The other is made
from stainless steel and plastic.
Which do you think is the modern one?

17

Cookers

Although some food can be eaten raw, most food is cooked before we eat it.

Range

A hundred years ago, many people cooked their food on a range, like the one in the picture below.
Ranges usually had one or more ovens, with some hot plates on the top.
The heat came from a coal or wood fire inside the range.

Gas

This is a gas cooker from the 1920s. It has an oven, a grill and some gas burners on the top.
In the twenties, many people used gas for lighting and cooking.
Few people had electricity in their homes.

Electricity

From the early 1930s onwards, electricity was supplied to more and more homes.

This picture of a 1950s electric cooker shows a woman setting the automatic timer, before going shopping with her friend.
Instead of having to make a fire, cookers could now be turned on and controlled with a few switches and knobs.

Today, many people have a microwave oven as well as a cooker.

Cooking

Who cooks your food for you?

Baking
This picture was taken in the 1890s.
The two women are baking bread in a bread oven, which was shared by all the people in the village.
Bread was cheap and filling.
Poorer people saved money by doing as much of their own baking as possible.

Cooks

People in well-off households often employed a cook to do all their cooking.

Meals took a long time to prepare as everything was home-made.

The cook in the picture on the right is choosing the day's meat from the butcher's delivery cart.

Cookery lessons

The girls in this 1930s photograph are having a cookery lesson at school.

Girls were expected to be able to cook, so that they could make meals for their husbands when they got married.

Today, many men, as well as women, enjoy cooking.

Cooking takes up less time, too, as we can buy ready-made meals and sauces.

Meals

Food is eaten at meal-times.

At home
The photograph on the right was taken in 1913. The family in the picture are having their tea in the garden.
Today, people sometimes use a barbecue to cook meals in their garden.
A maid is serving this family.
Who serves your meals?

At work
The photograph on the left was taken in a coal mine in the 1940s. The miners have stopped work to eat their lunch. Today, many workers eat their lunch in a canteen.

At school

These children are eating their lunch at school.
After the Second World War, all children were given free school meals
to make sure that everyone had at least one hot meal a day.
Today, some children have a hot school lunch and others have a packed lunch.
What sort of lunch do you have at school?

Glossary

artificial fertiliser a mixture, made in a factory, that improves the soil

automatic works by itself

churns large containers in which milk is stored

compartment separate section

employed paid to do work

Formica a special sort of plastic-type covering

pesticides chemicals that kill animals that destroy crops

rationing the sharing out of food

scattering sprinkling in all directions

Second World War a war fought between 1939 and 1945

transporting carrying from one place to another

Index

Timeline

nearly 120 years ago	nearly 110 years ago	nearly 100 years ago	nearly 90 years ago	nearly 80 years ago	nearly 70 years ago	nearly 60 years ago	nearly 50 years ago	nearly 40 years ago	nearly 30 years ago	nearly 20 years ago	nearly 10 years ago
the 1880s	the 1890s	the 1900s	the 1910s	the 1920s	the 1930s	the 1940s	the 1950s	the 1960s	the 1970s	the 1980s	the 1990s
1880	1890	1900	1910	1920	1930	1940	1950	1960	1970	1980	1990

How to use this book

Each book in this series takes a familiar topic or theme and focuses on one area of the curriculum: science, art and technology, geography or history. The books are intended as starting points, illustrating some of the many different angles from which a topic can be studied. They should act as springboards for further investigation, activity or information seeking.

History
changes have taken place during the past one hundred years, relating to:
- the way food is produced
- how food is transported
- where and how food is bought
- the variety of food available
- the utensils used to prepare food
- how food is cooked
- where food is stored
- how food is preserved
- eating meals

FOOD
key concepts and activities explored within each book

Art and Technology
- food is prepared to make it taste good and look attractive
- chefs are creative with food
- some tools are especially designed for food
- food features in 'still life' works of art
- make a pizza
- design a menu
- print with food
- model a meal
- create a summer drink
- make a still life picture

Science
- all living things need food
- plants make their own food
- foods can be classified into different groups
- we need to eat a variety of foods
- our bodies use different types of food in different ways
- a healthy diet is important
- food travels through our digestive system
- smelling and tasting food involves our senses
- food changes when it is cooked or heated

Geography
- food is usually produced on farms
- there are different types of farm, where different types of food are produced
- climate and land-type determine the food produced
- food can be found in salt water and fresh water
- many foods are processed and packaged in factories
- food is sold in markets, supermarkets and shops
- food can be imported and exported